Dear Parents,

Welcome to the Scholastic Reader series. We have taken over 80 years of experience with teachers, parents, and children and put it into a program that is designed to match your child's interests and skills.

Level 1—Short sentences and stories made up of words kids can sound out using their phonics skills and words that are important to remember.

Level 2—Longer sentences and stories with words kids need to know and new "big" words that they will want to know.

Level 3—From sentences to paragraphs to longer stories, these books have large "chunks" of texts and are made up of a rich vocabulary.

Level 4—First chapter books with more words and fewer pictures.

It is important that children learn to read well enough to succeed in school and beyond. Here are ideas for reading this book with your child:

- Look at the book together. Encourage your child to read the title and make a prediction about the story.
- Read the book together. Encourage your child to sound out words when appropriate. When your child struggles, you can help by providing the word.
- Encourage your child to retell the story. This is a great way to check for comprehension.
- Have your child take the fluency test on the last page to check progress.

Scholastic Readers are designed to support your child's efforts to learn how to read at every age and every stage. Enjoy helping your child learn to read and love to read.

> **—Francie Alexander**
> Chief Education Officer
> Scholastic Education

For my brother, Kevin, who's definitely a little odd
—K.C.

To Leal
—H.M.

Library of Congress Cataloging-in-Publication Data is available.

ISBN 0-590-22715-7

10 9 8 7 6   05 06 07
Printed in the U.S.A.   23
First printing, April 1996

Even Steven and Odd Todd

by Kathryn Cristaldi
Illustrated by Henry B. Morehouse

Scholastic Reader — Level 3

Cartwheel
·B·O·O·K·S·®

SCHOLASTIC INC.
New York   Toronto   London   Auckland   Sydney
Mexico City   New Delhi   Hong Kong   Buenos Aires

Even Steven lived on the edge of town
in a two-story house
with a four-bicycle garage.
He had six cats,
eight gerbils,
ten goldfish,
and a flower garden with twelve sprinklers.

"I'll have two loaves of bread,"
said Even Steven when he went to the bakery.
At the library he checked out four books.
At the post office he bought eight stamps.
Even Steven loved everything to be even.
"There's nothing odd about him,"
his neighbors told each other.

One day Even Steven heard a knock
on his door. He looked out the window.
It was Cousin Odd Todd.
Even Steven pulled down the shade
and turned off the lights.
"No one is home!" he shouted.

He heard three knocks.

He heard five knocks.

Then he heard seven knocks.
"Stop! Stop!" Even Steven
cried out twice.
He opened the door.

"Odd Todd," said Even Steven.

"What a surprise."

"Hey, Cuz!" came a voice from behind
three odd-shaped suitcases.

"Guess who is spending the summer with you?"

Even Steven looked up and down the street.
He looked behind the bushes.
He looked under the welcome mat.
He did not see anyone.
Except Odd Todd.
It was going to be one LONG summer.

The next morning Even Steven got up
at 8 o'clock sharp.
He was very hungry.
"I will make pancakes for breakfast," he said.
"If I make four pancakes,
I can have two now and save two for lunch.

"If I make eight pancakes,
I can have four now
and save four for lunch."
Even Steven smacked his lips.
Counting pancakes made him
very, very hungry.

He decided to make twelve pancakes.
Six for now and six for lunch.

Just then Odd Todd woke up.
It was 9 o'clock sharp.
"Yum, I smell pancakes," he said.
Odd Todd rubbed his stomach
thirteen times.

He went into the kitchen.

Even Steven was washing his plate.

He did not see his cousin.

CHOMP! CHOMP! CHOMP!

"Good morning, Cuz," said Odd Todd,
with his mouth wide open.
Even Steven's mouth fell open, too.
He stared at the plate of pancakes.
Now there were only three
odd pancakes for lunch.
"What's so good about it?"
Even Steven snapped.
He went out to work in his garden.

Even Steven loved his garden
more than anything.
"Today I will plant six rows of petunias,
eight rows . . ."
HONK! HONK! HONK!
Even Steven looked up.

Odd Todd rode by on a tricycle
with three wheels,
five different-colored streamers,
and a horn shaped like a parrot.
Odd Todd waved with one hand.
He was not watching where he was going.
Odd Todd rolled straight into
Even Steven's garden!

Even Steven's face turned beet-red.
Two puffs of smoke came out of his ears.
"My prize four-leaf clovers!" he shouted.
"Look what you have done!"
"I'm really, really, really sorry,"
Odd Todd said.
"I'll buy you lunch," he added.
Even Steven thought it over.
It was almost noon.
Odd Todd could not get into trouble
as long as they were together.
The pair of cousins headed for town.

Even Steven and Odd Todd
went to the pizza place.
"I would like four slices," said Even Steven.
"Two with onions and two with olives."
"I would like three slices," said Odd Todd.
"One plain, one with extra cheese,
and one with gummy worms."

Even Steven looked at his cousin's pizza.
There were nine pink worms on it.
Nine squishy, wiggly worms.
His face turned green.
"You look a little pale, Cuz," said Odd Todd.
"You should get out in the sun more."

Even Steven and Odd Todd
walked to the ice-cream shop.
"I will have two scoops of double-dip
chocolate chocolate," said Even Steven.
"I will have a triple nutty fudge sundae,"
said Odd Todd. "Extra nuts, please."
Even Steven went to look for a seat.
Odd Todd brought the ice cream.

Even Steven took a bite of his ice cream.
Then he saw something odd. It was the nuts.
There were exactly eleven.
"Nuts!" he screamed.
"Who put nuts on my double-dip
chocolate chocolate?"

Even Steven's face turned blue.
Four puffs of smoke came out of his ears.
"No need to thank me, Cuz." Odd Todd smiled.
"They were extras."

On the way home Even Steven saw a sign
in the flower shop.

Perfect Garden

Contest

BIG PRIZE

"I have a perfect garden," said Even Steven.
"It's perfect because it's perfectly even."

He wrote his name on the contest list.
"Hey, Cuz, check out this plant," said Odd Todd.
Even Steven did not answer. He ran home
and turned on his twelve sprinklers.
Then Even Steven took a nap.
He dreamed about winning the big prize.

Even Steven woke up and went
to his perfect garden.
The contest judge would be coming soon.
Even Steven counted his six rows of petunias,
his eight rows of daisies,
his ten rows of sunflowers,
and . . . one row of cactuses!
Each cactus had five long, sharp needles!
Even Steven's face turned purple.
Six puffs of smoke came out of his ears.

"That's it!" Even Steven screamed.
"I can't take you anymore, Cousin!
You are too odd!"

Just then the contest judge came over
to the garden.
"Odd, hmmm, yes. But I like it!
We have a winner!"

He handed Even Steven two tickets.
Two tickets to Twin Lakes!
Even Steven smiled.
"Now who shall I take on this trip for two?"
he asked.
"Don't worry, Cuz," Odd Todd said.
"My three bags are already packed!"

ABOUT THE ACTIVITIES

Words used in mathematical contexts often have different meanings when used in "regular" English. The word *even*, for example, is used in many different ways: "We shared the candies and it came out even." "Watch your step, the sidewalk isn't even!" "Put in even amounts of flour and water." The same with *odd*: "That's an odd name." "There are 300-odd pages in the book." "I found an odd sock in the drawer."

Mathematically speaking, however, *even* and *odd* have very precise meanings that children need to learn. And children learn about the mathematical meanings of words the same way they learn about all words — by hearing them used in contexts and using those words themselves. Also, because mathematical ideas are often abstract, it helps to teach children about "even" and "odd" by using physical materials.

The activities and games in this section present different ways to think about even and odd numbers. The activities also show examples of even and odd numbers in real-world contexts. The directions are written for you to read along with your child. You'll need counters for three of the activities; pennies, buttons, beans, or any other small objects will do.

The activities appeal at different levels of under-standing. Try a different activity at each reading. Be open to your child's interests, and have fun with math!

— Marilyn Burns

You'll find tips and suggestions
for guiding the activities whenever
you see a box like this!

Retelling the Story

Even Steven likes only even numbers: 2, 4, 6, 8, 10, 12, and so on. Do you know some even numbers that come after 12?

Odd Todd likes only odd numbers: 1, 3, 5, 7, 9, 11, 13, and so on. Do you know some odd numbers that come after 13?

What even numbers of things did Steven have? Check back in the story to help you remember.

When Odd Todd came to visit Even Steven, he knocked on the door. How many times did he knock? How else did Odd Todd show he liked odd numbers? Look in the book to find out.

Be a Number Checker

Here are four ways to check if numbers are even or odd. List the numbers from 1 to 20. Then check each number, using any of the four ways. Write "even" or "odd" to show what you found out.

Some children will notice the pattern that even and odd numbers alternate. Others will choose to test each number, often in no special order, and not notice the pattern until later.

#1. Two-Handed Grab

Pick a number. Put that many counters in a line. Put your hands into position, one at each end of the line. Say, "Ready, go!" and grab a counter from each end. Place the counters you grabbed in front of you.

Put your hands back at the ends of the line. "Ready, go!": grab two more. Keep going until you've either grabbed them all or there's one counter left over. If you have a counter left over, that means you started with an odd number. If you grabbed them all, the number is even.

#2. Two by Two

Take some counters and line them up, two by two. Is there a counter without a partner? Then the number you started with is odd. If they all have partners, the number is even.

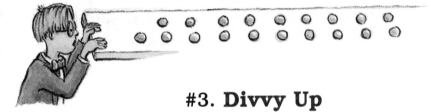

#3. Divvy Up

Take two sheets of paper. Take some counters and divvy them up so there is the same amount on each sheet of paper. Count to be sure. If you have a leftover counter, the number you started with is odd. If you shared them evenly, then the number is even.

#4. Count by 2's

When you count by 2's, (2, 4, 6, 8 and so on), all the numbers you say are even. If you don't say a number when you count by 2's, that means it's odd.

It's an Even, Odd World!

Sometimes it matters whether a number is even or odd. Take house numbers, for instance. What's your house number? Is it even or odd? On most streets, houses with even numbers are on one side; those with odd numbers are on the other side. Why do you think we use this system?

Animals always have an even number of legs. Birds have two legs; dogs and cats have four legs; and spiders have eight legs. There aren't any animals that have an odd number of legs. What other animals can you think of? How many legs does each have?

Think about wheels. Bicycles have two wheels — an even number. Odd Todd's tricycle had three wheels. What about the number of wheels on cars? Trucks? Airplanes? Tractors? Scooters? Buses?

What things can you think of that always come in even numbers or odd numbers?